Prime Time

Prime Time

Poems by

William Heath

Cover design by Shay Culligan
Cover artwork by Joseph Caminals
Author photo by William Heath

ISBN: 979-8-90146-822-7
Library of Congress Control Number: 2026936263

Kelsay Books
502 South 1040 East, A-119
American Fork, Utah 84003
Kelsaybooks.com

for Mercé and Paul Tibbets,
good friends for many years

Other Books by William Heath

Prose

The Children Bob Moses Led (Milkweed Editions, 1995; paperback, 1997) is about the civil rights movement in MS. Awards: Hackney Literary Award for Best Novel (winner), National Book Award (nominee), Pulitzer Prize (nominee), and Ainsfield-Wolf Award (nominated by Joyce Carol Oates). *Time* magazine selected it as one of eleven outstanding novels on the African American experience. A 20th anniversary edition was published by NewSouth Books in 2014.

Blacksnake's Path: The True Adventures of William Wells (Heritage Books, 2008). Awards: James Fenimore Cooper Award (nominee) and History Book Club (Alternate Selection).

Devil Dancer (Somondoco Press, 2013) is a neo-noir crime novel set in Lexington, KY.

William Wells and the Struggle for the Old Northwest (U. of Oklahoma Press, 2015; paperback, 2017). Spur Awards (best history book and best first nonfiction book) and Oliver Hazard Perry Award (military history).

Heath also edited *Conversations with Robert Stone* (University Press of Mississippi, 2016; paperback, 2018).

Poetry

The Walking Man (Icarus Books, 1994) collects the best of the poetry he began publishing in the '60s. James Wright said of this early work: "William Heath is in my opinion one of the most brilliantly accomplished and gifted young poets to appear in the United States in quite some time. I am especially moved by the delicacy and precision of the language, which indicates a distinguished intelligence, and by the purity and depth of feeling in his poems." Richard Wilbur noted: "*The Walking Man* is the work of a poet who knows how to tell a story."

Steel Valley Elegy (Kelsay Books, 2022), selects his work set in the U.S., including poems from his chapbook *Night Moves in Ohio* (Finishing Line Press, 2019). Kit Hathaway noted that these poems "are by turns poignant, funny, and starkly realistic, teeming with fascinating storyline detail and imagery." Eamon Grennan added, "These poems are savvy and lively, as exact as a high jumper's focus, quick and accurate as a tennis player's eye, wrist, ankle. Heath's own remembrance of things past—an autobiography in miniature lit by the laser-light of memory."

Going Places (Kelsay Books, 2023), set abroad, is the companion volume to *Steel Valley Elegy.* The poems display an eye for telling detail; a lucid perspective; an ironic, witty, thoughtful sensibility; sonorous words; memorable narrative; a deft way of moving a poem down the page. Esperanza Hope Snyder stated, "William Heath is a master of describing his journeys to exotic and challenging places in the world, where people, history, art, and natural beauty inspire his poetry. Few poets understand the fragility of the world as deeply as Heath does."

Alms for Oblivion (Kelsay Books, 2024) contains autobiography, social commentary, travels, the natural world, the art of poetry, aging, and death. George Belgere said, "The poems have a lapidary precision in their intelligence and power of observation. Heath's lines lift me out of my own self-absorption and into a larger world. He has an emphatic awareness of what it means to be human. Reading this marvelous collection reminds me of why I came to poetry in the first place."

Inventing the Americas (Finishing Line Press, 2024) is a chapbook on Columbus and Vespucci ideal for classroom use. Zeese Papanikolas noted, "'The world in his head / is not the one under his feet,' Heath says of Columbus. He tells the story of European conquest of this land with a poet's eye, finding just the right moment, the right detail to distill this tale of exploitation, enslavement, and death into 13 concise poems."

Acknowledgments

My thanks for their invaluable suggestions and assistance to Frank and Holly Bergon, Marty Malone, David Salner, to David Stevenson for providing his fine blurb, and most of all to my beloved co-conspirator, Roser Caminals-Heath.

Gratitude to the following publications, where versions of these poems previously appeared or are forthcoming:

All the Men Came & Danced (anthology, Wyld Syde Press, 2025): "Big Man on Campus," "A Trip to Montreal," "Prime Time"
Adelaide: "Happy Hour," "A Boy's Life," "Good (or Bad) Samaritan?"
American Writers Review: "I Am Not a Robot"
The Big Windows Review: "The Tattoo Artist"
Book of Matches: "Sir Humphrey Gilbert Sets Sail"
Chaos & Flowers (anthology, Cork City, Ireland): "The Critic"
Exit 13: "Tom Paine's Bones"
The Dead Mule School of Southern Literature: "Tales from Liberty"
Euphony Journal: "La Te Da"
The Font: "Lit Crit"
The Galway Review: "Men's Book Club," "Bass Man," "Walt and the Supremes," "Prime Time," "Who's Crazy Now?" "High Tea at Avebury," "Apartment Hunting in Lexington," "Jimmie and Sook," "Green Haven," "Big Jim," "Drive-in Dreams," "Curmudgeon's Lament" "The Poison Kitchen," "A House in the Country," "An Accident," "New England," "Welcome to Scotland"
Harbour Lights: "The Split-Up," "In Those Days," "Chopsticks," "Dining Alone," "Suburban Rites," "Chesapeake Shellfish"
In Parenthesis: "Cityscape," "Memories of Magdalen," "The Poet in New York," "No Pain Like the Back"

Lost Pilots: "Mixed Drinks and Metaphors"
MacQueen's Quinterly: "Augustine's Erections" [Pushcart nominee]
Memoryhouse Magazine: "Remembering My Father"
Mid-Atlantic Review: "Horses and War," "Punk Rock"
Midwest Quarterly: "Irreconcilable Differences," "Take a Walk"
Night Moves in Ohio, a chapbook (Finishing Line Press): "The Saywell Side" "Kissing Games in Ohio"
North American Review: "Lear on the Heath"
North Dakota Quarterly: "The Need for Trees," "The Spin on Things"
Northern New England Review: "A Thanksgiving Tale"
Penmen Review: "Orderly Chaos," "A Farm in Ohio," "The Easy Life"
Pennsylvania Literary Journal: "Killer Whales Attack Yachts Off Gibraltar"
Perceptions: "Of Books and Bombs"
Pulsebeat: "If Dogs Were Poets," "Jay and Eddie," "London Underground"
Qwerty Magazine: "Diogenes," "Pythagoras"
Slant Poetry: "Grace on Skates"
Stillwater Review: "Descartes"
Talking River Review: "The Stickup"
Tipton Poetry Journal: "The Connoisseur," "Virginia"
The Umbrella Factory: "The Invention of Immortality," "On the Afterlife," "Three Takes on Immortality"
Washington Writers' House: "Lot's Wife"

Contents

Part V: Curmudgeon's Lament

What shocks the virtuous philosopher
delights the chameleon poet.
—John Keats

Part I:
Boy Up a Tree

The Saywell Side

Mom's parents won't let Dad
stay in the house; lacking cash
for a hotel, he sleeps on the floor

of a laundry room at the back,
sneaks out before dawn to avoid
running into Mom's mother.

George Saywell fancies himself
upper crust, but after the Great
Crash he can't wing it, never

invites his high-toned friends
to their home in Hudson,
calls it "a miserable hovel."

Every Sunday he goes golfing.
Mom's mom, in an early photo
with her sisters, looks pensive.

Nobody knows for sure what kills
Fanny's spirit. She becomes colorless,
dresses drably, is an inept cook,

detests meat. She wears her hair
in a snug bun, takes little interest
in anything, stays in her room.

She never allows her daughter
in the kitchen, so when Mom
marries Dad she can't cook.

When Fanny's mind and body
fail, to pay for her final care
George must sell the house.

Mom and Dad

Dad, striving to rise above
his salt-of-the-earth farmer heritage,
marries Mom, the intellectual
daughter of an English-born patent
attorney in Cleveland. After
the divorce he returns to his
down-home ways, marries
his secretary, Louise II, who
always sings his praises.

Mom,
with her patrician Hudson, Ohio,
upbringing, Oberlin education,
is a devout Methodist, loves
to attend Sunday services, is
highly suspicious of Catholics.
She warns me of the dangers of
marrying my Catholic high-school
sweethearts, Carol and Betty.

After Dad leaves she goes door
to door selling Avon products,
meets and marries Guido. They
take turns listening to a sermon
or attending mass, while I come
home from Spain with Roser,
my Catholic bride from Barcelona.
What we most believe in is
each other and literature.

Remembering My Father

If my dad dies a few years
before the divorce, while I am
fifteen, say, a sophomore obsessed
with breasts and basketball,
I'll remember our summer vacations,

our trips to Virginia and New England,
historical sites like Fort Ticonderoga,
what he says to Mom the few times
he breaks through her monologues.
How he looks: a tall, dark-haired man,

a tad overweight, with long strong legs,
rock-solid calves. The mornings he drives
us boys on Lee Run Road to Poland High
(once the car on an icy road skids,
spins around twice before we stop)

on his way into Youngstown where he
serves as principal after years as
the assistant responsible for paddling
the day's worst offenders. On one
rare visit to his office he pulls out

a drawer packed with weapons:
switchblades studded with glass gems,
handmade knives scraped sharp on stones,
a zip gun wrapped in black electrical tape.
Two wooden paddles drilled with holes

to sharpen the smack hung on the wall
behind his desk. Each day he hits boys
my age who have misbehaved, each
evening he comes home, and no matter
what I do, only spanks me twice.

Boy Up a Tree

I used to climb a tall elm
that shaded our house
and look down on the whole
neighborhood. It was far
more dangerous than a boy
my age could realize, yet
limber branches near the top
held my weight as I swayed
in the breeze. An exhilarating
feeling that sent a tingle in

a place drawing more
of my attention. This was
before the time I invented
masturbation and kept it secret
from all the other boys
on Lee Run Road. I didn’t
climb the tree for that reason,
it was merely an off shoot of
the thrill of it all. Here I was
a small boy in a tall tree
lording it over the entirety
of the known world.

Character Is Fate

At Boy Scout camp I lie belly-down
on the ground, the butt of a .22 rifle
pressed to my shoulder, and pop
away at a not-so-distant target set up
on a hillside. I'm good enough to receive
a sharpshooter patch for Mom to sew

on my uniform, and I'm not bad at
pulling back a bow string to stick
arrows in an upended bale of hay.
I know how to tie more than my
share of intricate knots and how
to shuffle through a rain dance.

I'm on my way up in this world
of badges and higher ranks,
Eagle Scout might be in my future,
until at one meeting I'm kicked
out for giggling nonstop during
the Pledge of Allegiance.

A Farm in Ohio

I remember Aunt Hazel's two-story
wooden farmhouse by the roadside,
the flat fields of Northwestern Ohio
stretching out in all directions until

they hit a tree line left on purpose
to block the wind. The barns are
a short walk from the house and
a rooster commands the area

where we park. My bedroom
is up very narrow wooden steps.
By the time I come down
for breakfast the workers

have been out for hours, almost
since dawn. When they return
after ten to eat, their meal
amounts to a hearty dinner:

meat, potatoes, corn on the cob,
pass the peas, string beans, freshly
baked rolls, and, at the end, pass
the cherry pie. In the cowshed

I watch bald-headed Uncle Ed,
a large, bony man with a wide smile
that displays his missing teeth,
straddle a one-legged stool to milk

a cow persistently swishing its tail
to keep off the flies, hitting him
on occasion in the face as he cusses.
I try my hand but barely get

a drop, squeeze harder and pull
he tells me, but at this rate it will
take all afternoon to fill a pail.
Later that day, sent on an errand

to the henhouse, I come back
with the glass egg. It isn't
hard to see I'm not cut out
for a farming life.

Kissing Games in Ohio

It starts in third grade. Girls
chase boys on the playground,
kiss whoever they catch.
By junior high we graduate
to Spin the Bottle. Down in
Wendy's basement rec room
we sit in a circle, a Coke bottle

in the center, taking turns.
The spin decides who is kissed.
Then comes Post Office, more
privacy, freedom to select.
A postmaster announces a letter,
postage due in the next room.
If the transaction lingers, loud

protests and doors thrown open.
At last Flashlight in the dark,
a couple caught by the beam *not*
kissing is handed the flashlight
that finally is killed. I recall pitch-
black wanderings, kissing some
plum-luscious lips, speaking

in tongues so to speak. I've always
wondered whose lips I tasted.
Sophomore year kissing games cease,
no more sharing. Couples parking
beside the lake to watch "submarine
races" now hold exclusive rights
to each precious kiss.

A Boy's Life

We chip in for gas
money, fight over
who rides shotgun,
not that we have any
lethal weapons long
before drive-by shootings
become de rigueur for
boys in the hood, we
joyride up and down

our Main Street since
it isn't called that for
no good reason.
No hamburger joint
to hang out at, no gals
on roller skates to take
our order, we don't
even have souped-up
jalopies to drag race.

This is Poland, Ohio,
man, back in the Fifties,
and not much is shaking,
just an occasional rumble
between our corner gang
and the one from a rival
town, Boardman, belts
and bicycle chains
the weapons of choice.

Drive-in Dreams

I use a chamois, the most
exotic word I know, to polish
the hood, its touch different
from any other texture.

Under a hot sun, some slick wax
seems to promise my eager
fingers all the delights of a night
at the drive-in where I don't

go to see the movie. In those
high school days I often try
to stretch a double into a triple
with vague thoughts of reaching

home plate, but the lovely girls
I date are too quick for me,
somehow they sense where my
hands are headed and set up

a roadblock before arrival,
and as much as we enjoy
the kissing part each fears
heavy petting could lead to

deep trouble. At least in
my case, girls wisely realize
that this boy is in too much
of a rush to be serious.

Mixed Drinks and Metaphors

Down the hill, across the creek,
I can hear the Poland High band
practicing its discordant notes
over and over again without
getting it quite right. That's
the human condition for you,
we're all a bunch of bunglers
stumbling and spilling a drink
at a party where we never get
the right words out when talking
to the lovely lady in the low-cut
dress with a flute of champagne
in one hand and a tiny crustless
wedge of a sandwich in the other.
Yes, that's life, Sinatra sings,
the more you try the more the girl
and the goal elude you. But, hey,
it's all one big party, there are
more fish in the sea, so don't
be afraid of wet hands because
drinks get mixed and metaphors
get spilled by clumsy guys
stuck with slippery fingers.

Apartment Hunting in Lexington

She lives in a columned mansion near
downtown Lexington that features
a historical plaque and rises above shot-
gun shacks on three sides. She shows us
the hall where they once rolled back
the carpet to dance, the dining table
for twelve, the painting of a mounted
Henry Clay leaving for Congress.
Since her husband died a leaking faucet
brought down plaster in the salon
and her cat, knocked silly by a swinging
door, has to be put down.

After her husband's funeral she
notes that no one keeps calling hours.
When a person died there were three
or four times people could stop by
to express sympathy. Now they only
have one time and it's short. Nobody
is taught how to care anymore. Nobody
wears mourning, black armband for men,
black hat and dress for women. You
stayed in mourning for a certain period,
depending on the relationship.

She lacks time and energy to clean
chandeliers that once sparkled
with icy fire, so she'll sell and move
to Florida. "Don't you die," she says,
her face wrinkled as a winter apple,
shaking a finger in our direction.

Her old mansion is marvelous, but
her husband is dead and everything
falls apart. “Don’t you die,” she warns,
(looking at my wife but speaking to me)
“or if you have to die, don’t die first.”

New York, New York

for Toby Olson

I recall the time Toby and Miriam
live on the not-so-upper West Side.
I park beside a fenced-in lot
a few blocks from their apartment.

We enjoy an evening of wine drinking
and poetry talking. It is well past
midnight when I return to my car.
Even from down the street I see

something is terribly wrong,
a strange tilt soon reveals all tires
missing, windshield shattered,
steering wheel stolen, front seat ripped

out, trunk burst open, a box gone of
first editions (invaluable to me, worthless
to thieves) for Tom Berger, who lives
in a Gramercy Park penthouse, to sign.

The lifted hood, like a mouth shouting
for help, no longer covers an engine.
At Toby's I call the insurance agent,
tell her my car has been stripped

and totaled. In an abrasive voice
reminiscent of my third-grade teacher
she scolds, "There's a big difference,
young man, between stripped and totaled."

I am aware of that and repeat
my assertion. She says tomorrow
a man will come make an estimate.
In the morning from across the street

I stare at the corpse of my Ford Falcon.
It seems I have parked in Spanish Harlem,
a boy from the neighborhood stands
on the roof as I watch and launches

a belly flop on the still-open hood,
smashing it down with a resounding crash
to the delight of his friends who take
turns lifting the hood and repeating

the stunt. A blind man comes tapping
down the sidewalk, stops, turns his head
toward the noise, reaches into the car
to snatch the ashtray, and taps away.

When the insurance man arrives
he opens his notebook, glances at
the damage, says in awe, "My god,
it really *is* stripped *and* totaled!"

Summer of the Wolf

That summer I study contemporary
American literature in a NEH seminar
led by Benjamin DeMott at Amherst.
The ten-bedroom country house where

I stay belongs to a professor on leave
in France. It seems many an Amherst prof
considers their salary, compared to trust
funds and stock holdings, pin money.

The highlight of the class is the day
a convert to performative feminism
takes the novel we are reading, tosses it
onto a platter at the center of our

seminar table, sets it on fire using her
cigarette lighter, strips to bra and panties,
and begins to dance with wild abandon
(abdomen?) beside the blaze.

I'm not sure what point she's making,
something about the male chauvinist authors
we've been reading and the way women
by nature long to run with the wolves.

As it so happens, a few evenings later
I am sitting on the veranda gazing
across an extensive lawn with a setting
sun in the distance and see what at first

looks like a large dog, yet something in
the way it moves and glances about
suggests a wolf on the prowl. But there
are no wolves in Massachusetts.

It is larger than a coyote and its coat
is gray. For decades I ponder the mystery
until recently I read a novel called *Happiness*
about an American woman who keeps track

of foxes living in London. In passing she
mentions that a few New England coyotes did
breed with wolves. That answers one question,
not the mystery of the dancing woman.

London Underground

On my first visit to London
the image that comes to mind
is of riding the escalator down

to and up from the Tube,
or Underground, far deeper
than the New York subway.

Most of the posters lining
the right-side wall during
descent and ascent aimed

at British men in raincoat,
bowler hat, rolled brolly,
who had mastered the art of

looking straight ahead while
gazing askance at the pulchritude
on display in ad after lingerie

ad of women in lacy bras.
As I went up and down I,
too, devoured those images

surpassing anything a Sears
catalogue had to offer
a growing boy in Ohio.

Memories of Magdalen College

Years ago I indulged in an Oxford
formal dining hall, beamed ceiling,
faded portraits on the walls, sipping
sherry with the dons before processing

to high table as undergraduates clatter
to their feet in their black gowns.
A short prayer in Latin, an anxious
wait for the warden to appear, then

the muffled racket of the students
as the multicourse meal is served.
Surprisingly for England, the wines
are superb, as well as sparkling cider

in a small engraved silver mug,
then brandies sampled in a side room
loosen the tongues of dons relating
fascinating tales of how research

took them to fascinating corners
of the globe. I confess a temptation to
filch a silver mug whose tiny dents
proclaim centuries of service.

High Tea at Avebury

High tea in the walled
garden of the vicarage,
not far from a circle
of stones I have come
to see, remnants of
a very old England far
from merry, yet intriguing.
The sun was the center
of worship in those times,
the huge stones placed
to capture its seasonal
movements in the sky.

But back to high tea,
a ritual so many Brits
find as irresistible as
their flower gardens,
and I do too. Who can
forget clotted cream
topped with jam, or is
it the other way around,
on a freshly baked scone?

And English tea from
a flower-patterned pot,
with a touch of milk,
a spoonful of sugar,
is the very definition
of a midafternoon pick-
me-up at the very hour
spirits and eyelids droop,
craving an infusion of
this perfect elixir.

A Trip to Montreal

My advice: don't try to drive
across Pennsylvania if stoned,
even a little, as Jim and I are
when we take my Datsun from
Ohio to Montreal to visit a high
school friend, another Jim.

Things turn freaking strange
when we see a buffalo herd
grazing in a pasture, then
we hit a town that goes on
mile after mile in an area
where no big cities exist.

It seems Williamsport backs
a mountain on one side and
straddles a river on the other
(no doubt a flood-prone place)
thus the large town consists
of one interminable street.

In those days draft-age guys
heading for Canada are suspect:
our tie-dyed T-shirts, flowing
hair, drooping mustaches
cause guards at the border
to question us, search the car.

We've toked our final joint
hours before, travel the last
many miles with windows down,
our deferments are valid, so we
keep on rolling into Montreal
and crash at my friend's pad.

That is the year of Expo 67,
built on a few expanded islands
in the Saint Lawrence, Bucky Fuller's
geodesic dome the centerpiece.
One structure, burned to the ground,
I dub the Vietnam pavilion.

Funny bit we agree, "black humor"
being an in thing then, but not a line
I'm proud of now. Jim lives with
a fiery French-speaking girl, they
take us to their log cabin getaway
where we swim in an icy lake.

Jim and his girl quarrel a lot
in two languages, adding spice
to their relationship. We feast
on tasty food, drink an inordinate
amount of wine, stay up late
talking about the good old days.

This is how buddies behaved
back then, probably still do,
for better or worse. Good times
if you're not old enough to know
what good times really are
or what life has in store for you.

On our return, Jim and I toss a Frisbee
as border guards search the car, spotting
a Styrofoam basket in the trunk packed
with towels and wet suits covering
a brown substance in a plastic bag:
pot smugglers caught red-handed.

One guard pours some in his hand,
rubs it for texture, takes a taste,
says, "Shit, it's fucking granola."

Welcome to Scotland

At Ullapool our guide has
sandy blond hair, a raspy voice,
and keen blue/green eyes.
Her fishing village of two-story
whitewashed houses faces
a long dock and runs three streets
deep before yielding to a rocky
hillside of pasture land for
grazing clusters of sheep.

For a thousand years the town
has lived off the sea's bounty:
"darling herring" the prime catch
as well as shrimp, cod, and other
tasty morsels of the deep. Nowadays
Spain is the main market, yet in the past
herring, packed in brine, fed slaves
on Caribbean plantations.

She thinks it a bad idea to send
salty food to people in tropical climes,
though sodium replenishes what
the body loses by sweating.
As for herself, she never eats
creatures that live underwater.
Surf & Turf is a one course meal.

How confident she is in her Scots
stubbornness, not a wee hint of doubt
in her firm position. You might think
a tour guide would be cosmopolitan
and open to new experiences,
yet her village is a prized spot for seafood
she has no intention to ever taste.

Part II:
Irreconcilable Differences

Jay and Eddie

Over the holidays we visit Katy's parents
in Durham, her father Jay is a mid-level
executive for a big tobacco company when
it first becomes beyond dispute that smoking
causes lung cancer. A tall, haughty, bourbon-
drinking man uneasy with himself.

The home is on a cul-de-sac backed
onto a swamp, their property including
the wetlands borders a dirt road where
Eddie and his wife live. Jay "rents"
for free a tar-paper shack to them, Eddie
reciprocates by doing a few odd jobs.

Jay and Eddie love to hunt together, set
muskrat traps. When Eddie comes by he
stoops down to knock on the bottom
half of the back door. Jay doesn't approve,
but Eddie is an old-timey kind of man
who always does it that way.

Jay and Jan's home is a larger, stylized
version of those weatherboard houses
common in the South before folks with
cash switch to brick. The main room features
a cathedral ceiling, stone fireplace, a balcony
leading to second floor bedrooms.

One day Jay, already drunk, tells me to come
with him to buy a gun from a man in a parking lot
on the other side of town, says he'll feel safer

not going alone. Jay returns from the sale,
gun in hand, blurts out he doesn't know what
he'll do if anyone mistreats his daughter.

Eddie is resourceful, constructing a tractor
from junkyard scrap metal and truck parts.
It looks strange, sort of like a grasshopper,
but it works. A cast iron stove keeps his home,
for me, uncomfortably hot. Pictures of a girl in
a graduation gown, JFK, and MLK on the wall.

On Christmas Eve, while Jay and Eddie shot-
gun mistletoe down from an oak in the swamp,
we sing carols at Duke's Gothic style cathedral.
Although he can't admit it, Jay's best friend
is a man who always, when he comes to visit,
knocks on the bottom half of his back door.

Tales from Liberty, Mississippi

1
At a Frederick, Maryland, art gallery
I meet a bearded painter working in pastels
from Liberty. He serves as a sniper
in Laos—tells me of killing a man, a village
organizer, on his front porch. He thinks
he might have to take out one or two of his kids
but he gets his man on the first shot, then
gives him three more to make sure.
Our Special Forces, he says, think nothing
of hacking off a man's head, sticking it on a pole
for the whole village to see, of walking around
with a girl's pubic hair on a helmet. That is how
the game is played and, he says, what's hard
to convey is how exciting it all is.

2
When he says his last name my heart jumps.
I ask about a relative I suspect shot Louis Allen
in his own driveway because he witnessed
state representative E. R. Hurst gun down
Herbert Lee—a local farmer helping Bob Moses
register voters—at a Liberty cotton gin.
"He is one mean piece of work," he says,
"his kids are mean too, mean as snakes,
they'd as soon shoot you as look at you."
The original relative, a thief in Scotland,
is smuggled here from Liverpool in a coffin.
The man I suspect is a police officer
in Alabama before he comes to Liberty.
A died-in-the-wool racist, he is part of
a hardcore group associated with
a four-square-gospel Baptist church.
The murder of Louis Allen is still unsolved.

Green Haven

for Frank Bergon

My friend Frank teaches creative writing
at Green Haven, the maximum security prison
halfway up the Hudson from New York.
I come with him sometimes to help
with poetry. Five hundred of the inmates,
mostly Black, are convicted murderers.

Frank tells his class concrete detail is
essential for good writing. One large
brooding guy sitting in the back breaks in:
"Excuse me, excuse me, if I took a shiv
and slit you from your gut to your throat
would that be *concrete* enough for you?"

It'd be concrete Frank concedes, keeping
his cool, but it wouldn't be good writing.
I give a talk about alliteration, assonance,
consonance, metrical forms, and so forth,
collect their drafts to read at home.

The next class Frank returns the pages
marked in red pen with my suggestions
to make the poems shorter and tighter.
"When is Heath and his knife coming back?"
an inmate asks after extensive revision.
"That man sure can cut." This reminds me

of Lotte Lenya in *The Threepenny Opera:*
Just a jackknife has Macheath, dear / And he
keeps it out of sight . . . / Fancy gloves, though,

wears Macheath, dear / And there's not a trace
of red. Yet I dread to know what the guy
sitting in the back feels about *his* cuts.

Our Vassar colleague Susan asks if she
can come with us, would it be safe?
One inmate, aka Money, offers protection.
Frank asks him what he's in for: "I saw
three cops beating up on my good buddy,"
Money explains. "I had to disable them."

For my course on Crime in America
I combine sociology and literature, focus
on criminal careers. Pickpockets and embezzlers
rarely commit rapes or muggings, and vice versa.
After Susan's successful visit I bring
my class, mostly women, to Green Haven.

We meet in a large hall and I give a brief talk,
ask and answer a few questions, then students
and inmates are free to mingle for discussions.
One Vassar coed is surrounded by men who
ask what "career" she's studying. "Rapists," she
replies. It seems they all are doing time for rape.

Later I learn that Green Haven is even more
dangerous than I assumed: endemic corruption,
a system of "favors" involving sex and drugs
lets inmates set terms, move about more freely.

In 1981, a few years after our class, a recently
hired female guard is lured to the office

of the chaplain and strangled by an inmate
doing three life sentences for raping and
murdering women. Her body wrapped
in trash bags is found in a landfill. She is
the first female corrections officer killed
on duty in United States history.

Her memorial headstone is now visible to all
who pass through Green Haven's iron gates.

The Stickup

Three men enter the bank, ski masks
over their faces. One, waving a semi-
automatic handgun at customers,
should have shouted, "On the floor,
motherstickers, this is a fuckup,"
given what happens. Shotgun in hand,
another jumps over the counter,
orders the tellers to stuff the money
in a plastic bag. The third eyes
a stopwatch to keep track of time.
You see these three-time losers
think the script of *Point Blank,*
a Patrick Swayze, Keanu Reeves flick,
holds the key to untold treasure.

My eighty-something father
having just cashed a check walks
toward the door. "They seemed nervous,"
Dad says later," so I kept on walking.
I didn't pay any attention to them,"
even when he is told to stop.
After a few steps the shortest one,
a nasty five-foot-six punk, shoves
him in the chest and down he goes.
Blood spreads when his skull smacks
the marble floor. The distraction
enables a teller to set off the alarm.

The thieves flee, forget to remove
their masks, ditch the getaway car.

A passerby sees the switch to
a Lincoln Continental, notes
the license plate. Cops close in.
Robbers don't resist. The pint-
sized guy, a habitual offender,
seven felonies on his rap sheet.
At the trial, his best defense is
his father sleeps with his sister.
After six stitches at the hospital,
Dad recovers his old self,
as hardheaded as ever.

Summer of the Sniper

During the summer of the beltway sniper,
tanking up at the gas station is fraught
with danger, as is taking a walk in any
neighborhood or a trip to the supermarket.
Descriptions of a white getaway van
prove to be false.

No one knows what the killers
look like or the color of the vehicle
they drive or where they might
strike next. As Marshall and I play
tennis at a Rockville park not far
from DC we often see a police car
circling the courts and baseball field.
You bet we feel the fear.

The two are finally caught, asleep
in their blue Caprice at a truck stop
off Route 70, a few miles from my
home in Frederick, their next target.
The teenage rifleman uses a hole drilled
in the trunk to pick off random victims.

The boy, under the influence of
an older man who plans to shoot
his ex-wife, gladly does as he is told.
All ten killings are intended as cover
for the one murder that will not
be a whim of fate.

A Thanksgiving Tale

It's a snowy Thanksgiving, roads are slick
on the way to Grandma's place
for a family reunion.

Upon arrival Ben the cop is directing
traffic since lines are down.
I step out of the car

to fetch the bowl of cranberry sauce
my wife has prepared
just as Uncle Joe's

SUV skids on ice, whacks my bumper,
the jolt sends me sliding under
the car into a ditch.

Need I say the bowl breaks, spewing
its crimson contents all over
my face and clothes

as the whole family shouts and cries
to see my bloody body
in the snowy ditch.

The cop rushes to the scene of the crash,
only to also slip into the ditch
and smack into my side

while I'm still in a daze from my fall.
"What the fuck!" I say as everyone
laughs at my return to normal,

except for Ben, muttering in bafflement.
I steady him to his feet and explain,
"It's cranberry sauce, Ben.
Happy Thanksgiving."

La Te DA

In Key West we go to the La Te Da
evenings after dinner, sip prosecco splits,
dance to live singers of varying merit,
some hiding their incandescence under
this obscure basket, others no more
than wannabes in the grand scheme.

A pool smaller than a paddleball court,
where a toothy inflated alligator drifts
with the ceiling fans, lies next to
the linen-covered dining tables.

The back of the waiter's black T-shirt
reads: *If you want to drink all day*
you must start in the morning.

The host sports his usual cowboy
hat and boots, Bermuda shorts,
smiles in recognition, locates seats
beside the small stage—it's over
a year since he's seen us—one more
reason we keep coming back.

Men's Book Club

They quit on *One*
Hundred Years of
Solitude in the first
chapter. I point out,
to no avail, the author
won the Nobel Prize
and his novel was
a huge bestseller on
several continents,
but they aren't having
any of that, they know
what they don't like.

What they go for are
blockbuster books,
The American Sniper
by a guy named Flynn,
the hero is CIA, kills
nefarious enemies on
a regular basis,
always finds a babe
to hop into bed with
even though they met
an hour before.

Flynn died years ago,
but not to worry
ghost writers crank out
Flynn-like novels that fly
off bookstore shelves.

The numbers of dead
bad guys incrementally rise
and isn't that a new babe

batting her eyes at our hero
in the hotel lobby?

I want to tell the men
in our book club that
this kind of crap is
the male equivalent
of Harlequin Romance,
only those are based on
the kind of sentimentality
females fall for: once it
was bare-chested Raoul
of the flowing hair, pecs,
plus yacht, nowadays it's
the empowered woman
holding a gun in both hands,
and choosing whether
to shoot or shack up.

The male version is
a formulaic macho fantasy
of being the toughest kid
on the block or foreign country
if you are a sniper for the CIA.
Despite impossible odds
you outwit all foes, bed any
babe that happens to come
your way. Yet sex is only
an afterthought, preferably
a quickie, since a real man
has a hit list to finish off
before calling it a day.

Of Books and Bombs

Some jobs consist of saying
the same thing over and over,
the stewardess assuring us
a thingamajig will drop from

the ceiling of the plane if we
feel a sudden need for oxygen,
the post office lady asking,
each time I send a book via

Media Mail, if my package
contains dangerous chemicals,
the kind I might use to make
a bomb. I reply, no, it's

a book, so I press *Continue,*
then hit *No.* Yet what I want
to say is some books *are* bombs,
but would she understand?

I Am Not a Robot

Recently my computer
has been asking me if
I am a robot. A question
I never asked it to ask,
who does it think it is,
I wonder, wasn't that
a robotic thing to do?

But my computer is
a stubborn son of a gun,
or a nerd who began his
rise to fame and fortune
in a family garage,
and by fortune I mean
billions into trillions.

I'm left with no choice
in order to belong to
this worldwide high-
tech club where every-
body loves each other,
or is it that everybody
hates and unfriends

each other? This leaves
me no choice, I'd say,
than to use my cursor
(as I am comprehensively
cursing) to check the god-
damned box like any
good robot would.

Who's Crazy Now?

Back in the day, people
who talked to themselves
on the streets were crazy.
Now they're no longer
institutionalized due to
some well-intentioned
reform that didn't turn

out as expected. If you see
people on the sidewalk *not*
talking to themselves,
or not staring at a dark object
in their hand the size of a cheap
paperback, they just might be
in a shrinking minority

who don't walk around with
an iPhone as their closest
companion. They might leave
the damn thing in their car
for use in an emergency.
They might be someone
like me.

The Language of Love

Our seemingly puritanical recoil from
a literal depiction of sex makes sense,
for what is physical love but a transformation
of the dialectic that preceded it?
At heart it is an act beyond words.

Its very essence is found in this: body
language replaces verbal exchange,
we return to the ground of being by passing
beyond the need for talk. Lovers asking
how it was for the other only shows

it wasn't right for them. If they had
truly been within their bodies, letting
each have its mutual say, there would be
no need, at the end, to ask for a report.
Everything would simply be clear.

Prime Time

My wife, I am sure of it,
is having an affair with a guy
who drives a truck, drops
by on a regular basis, leaves
her nicely packaged presents

on our front porch. I bring
them in to hand over to her
and don't stand around until
they're opened. I want to be
discreet about all this, we're

both mature adults. I respect
her freedom and independence,
so we don't talk about it.
I swallow my pride, yet dread
the next day, his next visit,

the cocky devil even rings
the doorbell, leaves his gift,
and drives away in the same
truck as always, the one
with *Prime* on its side.

Irreconcilable Differences

My wife and I are now divorced
for a week due to irreconcilable
differences: she has Covid,
I don't. So it comes to pass we sleep
in separate beds, eat meals at
separate tables, read our books,
work at our computers, watch
television shows every evening
in different rooms. She is taking
Paxlovid and still has a few days
to go. At night in bed I hear

from the next room her occasional
cough, probably she hears me
make my nightly treks to the toilet
every few hours to pee. We hope
to work out a reconciliation soon
without the help of counseling.
A day will come when all the Paxlovid
pills are gone along with those
occasional coughs, the sinuses
will clear, and Covid will move on
to the next unlucky couple.

No Pain Like the Back

Don't talk to me about
the dark side of the moon,
a place none of us will
ever see. What bothers me
is my own back, it itches
where I can't scratch.

I feel a bump or two I can
not see: a cyst, a pimple,
or just some whim of my
skin that might go away
when I shower. Then,
on rare occasions, comes

a horrific shooting pain,
when it hits no agony is
as bad as lower back pain
which twice rushes me
to the hospital where I plead
for more morphine.

Take a Walk

It seems simple enough:
one foot in front of the other,
just as Lao Tse advises
a wise man to live. All it takes
is one small step for a man
(a giant leap for mankind)
even if you're not standing
on the moon.

When young I have a high-
jumper's bounce to my stride,
I love to stretch out my legs,
it gives me great pleasure
to walk as fast as I can.
If I am with a group I like
to act as an advance scout
scanning out prospects ahead.

What the rest think, no doubt,
is that I am simply being rude,
standoffish, striving to get one
up on everyone else, acting
like the Emperor of Japan,
not willing to slow down
and talk. True, I've often
been something of a loner
going my own way.

My wife Roser with her strong
agile legs strives to keep up,
and if I wrap an arm around
her waist we manage to maintain
a rapid pace—surely you can see
where this is headed for a once-
upon-a-time fast walker.

An old man now, my knees
are bone on bone, my thighs
prefer a recliner to a brisk walk
around the block. Now it's Roser,
a firm grip on my arm, who slows
down to fit my snail's crawl,
my small steps for a time.

Part III:
Grace on Skates

Grace on Skates

The best skaters glide
backwards on the ice
more swiftly than forward,
short skirts whipping
lithe legs.

This skating in reverse
is a kind of miracle
as if the act made time
go backwards too. She
already looks young,

but could I see her
become younger yet?
I think so. Perhaps it is
a secret of ice skaters,
why skating backwards

is grace in motion,
a defiance of the laws
of life, no wonder when
she leaps and spins
suspended a moment

in the air, time and gravity
in abeyance, I can even
believe the world ceases
to turn, stands still before
our mundane lives resume.

Lot's Wife

Of course I looked back,
who wouldn't? I'd left
friends and loved ones
behind in the doomed city,

site of many good times
and happy memories.
I didn't want to travel
those long dusty roads

with my drab husband.
I was sick of his pious
ways. Live a little, I
told him, there's a party

tonight. "There's a party
every night," he said
with his usual snarl, "I
don't like loud music."

The Critic

Even at an early age
she held herself apart.
Unlike the others
sharing the same opinions
hers were different,
what we would call
edgy, they had bite,
might be abrasive,
didn't go over too
well on dates.

Some days she felt
like a safecracker
sandpapering his
finger tips because
she did feel a click
when faced with
a real work of art,
the hair tingled
on top of her head.

What's the point,
she wondered,
to all these fine-tuned
discriminations?
What a farce to parse
the botched sentences
of the tone-deaf,
like a surgeon fingering
a poor soldier's gut
for shrapnel.

The critic is like
Emily Dickinson's father
ringing the church bell,
summing the reluctant
people of Amherst to gather
on the village green
to witness
a splendid sunset.

The Connoisseur

I make a point of standing
a considerate amount of time
before a painting—as if in
a studio, the painter in his

smock of many colors
waiting for me to make
pleasing comments.
If it's a portrait I know

not to say the mouth's not
quite right, if a landscape
to refrain from stating it's
just like such-and-such

a place I've seen before.
Maybe I'll settle for a little
mood music, as in the you-
make-me-feel-like song,

come up with an appropriate
emotion; if I don't like
the painting I do my best
to leave as quickly as

possible so that the gifted
artist, as least in his or her
own eyes, can get on with
the work in progress.

Artists and Cathedrals

When I visit the cathedrals
of Europe I often admire
the artist more than the art.
After all he, it was always
a *he* in those days, worked

under compulsion to paint
or fit the stained glass
of the windows with a set
of Biblical stories. The best
did their best to put in

a personal touch, a signature,
enough to show their figures
are not like those of every
other artist's people, faces
show genuine emotions,

telltale gestures, skilled
placement is an argument
for design. I also assume
if they are true artists that
in their souls at least a few

knew that all that Biblical
stuff wasn't true. The only
afterlife, at least for a time,
comes from being a person
who knows how to paint,

how to perfectly place
fragments of glass into
a mosaic that makes colors
come alive and a window
a thing of lasting beauty.

Of Time and Oils

An old painting going back
a century of a blonde flapper
in a bob cut, her loose-fitting
gown leaving her right arm bare,
an anything goes boo-boo-da-
doop look in eyes shadowed
like an Egyptian queen.

The aging oils now cracked
in so many places the painting
resembles those mosaics
Romans crafted to depict flappers
of their day: ladies in loose-
fitting gowns holding hands on high
to dance in a celebratory circle.

In Those Days

Back then couples court in buggies.
The parents pretend the beau
will have to devote his hands
to directions, but those horses know

their way around, and the whip
socket is an ideal place to wrap
the reins. You'd be surprised
at what hanky-panky went on

in a moving buggy. Not everyone
is a gentleman you know. I've
seen some terrible cads. One
young man in particular my father

finds out about and when he comes
to call denounces him as a cur
and tells him not to darken our
doorstep again. We didn't tolerate

certain things in those days. If
it is discovered your behavior
is not correct, you are banned.
Where once I had dimples now

you see wrinkles. When I first
learn how to drive a car I pull
back on the steering wheel, yell,
"Whoa" to make it stop.

Walt and the Supremes

The supernatural of no account, myself waiting
my time to be one of the supremes.
—Song of Myself 41

Walt predicted it and I'm sure
he'd fit right in if he shaved
his beard, permed his hair into
an Afro to match Diana Ross.

He'd have to lose a few pounds
and find a long sequined gown
to go with the other vocalists
strutting their stuff on the stage.

I have some doubts whether
his barbaric yawp would blend
in with the group, but he was always
a singer, even if his songs were
rather self-centered. If iPhones

had existed at the time I'm sure
he would have taken more than
his share of selfies, but we're
talking about great music here,
whether on the stage or page,

and Walt certainly belongs
among the Supremes.

The Poet in New York

The moment I step out
of the subway the people
of Manhattan always

recognize me, they honk
their horns incessantly
and in the distance I hear

sirens heading my way,
and every time I wave
my hand a yellow car

pulls up to the curb,
offers to take me any-
where I want to go as

we speed up the avenue,
and when on a whim
I hop out at a red light

he, too, honks his horn
real loud to wish me
one more happy visit.

Happy Hour

In this town as well as many
others across our great land,
Happy Hour is mandatory.
A posted sign in the window
of almost every bar declares
at this time you must cheer up,
have a beer or two or three,

smile into the foaming mug
if you've got enough sense,
as most guys don't, to savor
the blend of beer and suds from
a frosted glass rather than chug
from a bottle that deprives
your lips of the full taste—

but maybe that's just me.
It's a point I won't argue since
there are a lot of large men
with bottle in hand who might
take umbrage, which is to say
swing at my fragile jaw or
smack me upside the skull

with one of those said bottles
I've been getting so snooty
about. I wonder if you must
have a happy hour what does
that say about the other twenty-
three? It's enough to make
a man weep in his beer.

The Great Wine Exchange

Let them eat grapes, I say,
but pick and press them first,
age them in fired-to-fit oak casks
from France if your cellar is here,
in American oak if your chateau

is in France. Is the logic behind this
exchange to support international
shipping and the lumber industry?
Perhaps it's intended to dupe
wannabe connoisseurs or justify

the high price of quality wines?
Either way you've got to put
your nose in play: an initial
sniff before shaking the glass
for a more aromatic whiff,

next taste a sample not to sip
but chew as if rinsing your teeth;
don't swallow but spit it out
into a special cup—what fun
is that? If you like the wine

and want to buy some bottles,
purchase a case in France and
ship it to California, or if you
live in Burgundy ship wine home
in crates from Sonoma.

Irish Pubs and Poetry

The sound of poetry
is upon me I announce
at me pub, lyrics for
everyone in the house

who has ears to hear,
yet I can't say the mates
do hear me. They make
such a din I swear the

worm-eaten ceiling
begins to shudder,
as has happened on
previous occasions

for hundreds of years.
That's how ancient this
foking pub is with
its standing-room-only

army of local bards back
from the old sod ready
to share their latest
dithyrambs and ditties.

Punk Rock

I’m going to sponsor a punk
rock concert: in exchange for
a ticket, everyone who comes
is given a musical instrument,
chairs on the stage so people
can sit and listen as well as play

favorite songs, but you say all
they’ll make is noise, cacophony
is the word. Precisely my point,
I reply. I once knew a guy who
formed a garage band named
Dow Jones and the Industrials,

their breakout songs, published
in *The Toe Jam Review,* were
“I Wanna Hold Your Hardon”
and “I Wish I Was in Dixie,”
the name of the homecoming queen
known to twirl a mean baton

at this school somewhere
in a Middle American suburb
with a lot of two-car garages
and more punks pounding their
drumsticks than drums, if you
know what I mean.

If Dogs Were Poets

If dogs wrote poems
how everything smells
would be central, the world
is a cornucopia of odors.
They would bark in bardic
voices that each ass has its

own signature, scratching
in the dirt and such can be
an intense pleasure. There's
nothing like a good bite
of ground beef, human
legs with their own flavor

usually aren't worth it,
except when you get
really pissed off at some
mailman or delivery boy
who gets your hackles up,
treats you like a dog.

Big Jim[1]

I am an artist. I make *the truth.*
—James Dickey

He says he is a fighter pilot,
that the thrill of dogfights with
his Japanese counterparts is
better than sex. In truth, after
failing preflight tests he flies
combat missions as a radar man,
receives a few Bronze Stars not
Purple Hearts or the Congressional
Medal of Honor as he asserts.
Nor is he in the air over Nagasaki
when the A-bomb is dropped
or part of Gen. Curtis LeMay's
horrific firebombing of Tokyo.
He writes some powerful poems
about World War II, but none,
as he implies, true to his life.

Home from the war he attends
Vanderbilt on the G. I. Bill, not
athletic scholarships; he does sub
in football, is a decent high
hurdler, not an All Southern
tailback nor a setter of records
yet to be broken in the 100 yard dash,
the high hurdles, or the broadjump.

Nor is he an archery champion
as he often boasts. He tells these

---

[1] "Big Jim" is based on Henry Hart's biography, *James Dickey: The World as a Lie,* and Christopher Dickey's memoir, *The Summer of Deliverance,* as well as conversations with fellow poets over the years.

tales to impress his fellow poets,
especially James Wright.

Novelist Pat Conroy, a young man
at the time, believes that Big Jim has
a rendezvous with destiny involving
a huge black bear on an island off
the South Carolina coast. In single
combat, with bow and arrows,
he will confront the beast and
only one of them will survive.

At lunch with Robert Lowell,
Dickey pulls up his shirt to show
a bandage on his back. Stooping
to drink in a mountain stream,
he says a bear bit him from behind
before he shoots it with an arrow.
"But the bear wasn't dead, Jim,"
Lowell says bemusedly. "If you
return to your office you will find
Robert Bly sitting on your desk."

On the set of *Deliverance* he confides
to each key member of the cast
in turn that everything in the novel
is true, which of course is false.

He and some friends do go on
a few canoe trips, never a treacherous
white water river. Any encounters
with local hillbillies are friendly.

He claims to be of good mountain stock,
a log cabin up in the holler, taught to hunt,
fish, play the banjo by his pa, yet he
grows up on Atlanta's Peachtree Street
and Buckhorn, a posh enclave. Not the scion
of the Coca-Cola fortune, instead an ad man
for the company and Lay's potato chips.

Dickey lies with such conviction
his fellow writers believe him,
critics cite his shamelessly inflated
resume, take him at his word
that he has dined with T. S. Eliot,
that in his extensive correspondence
with Pound the famous poet tells him
his poems are the best he's read
since he discovered Robert Frost.

These tall tales are also his way
to bed as many women as possible,
preferably naïve coeds picked up
during his frequent campus readings.
Women are fair game, a perk to add
to his extravagant fees. His opening line:
"Are you fucking anyone regular?"

Lit Crit

Once students were taught
to look for symbolism,
almost anything, in their eyes,
stood for something else.

This kind of displacement
often led to bad reading,
the student was abstracted
away from the particulars

of the text—the actual images
and specific behavior of
the characters—into a realm
of misleading concepts that

were a total perversion of
the book's meaning. Nowadays
a PC reading does similar
damage—students play

gotcha with characters
and authors and the texture
of the work is torn
beyond recognition.

A Lesson in Diction

There is so much not
to say, often silence
is best, pithy Anglo
Saxon is preferable to
ornate Latinate words
although the latter, at least
in classroom usage, are
deemed more correct,
politically speaking.
Something I do not
strive to achieve ever
since I retired, leaving
students to jump through
other professors' hoops.
After a while you tire
of "What do I have
to do to get an A in
your class?" To which
one Kenyon professor
replied, "You must live
your whole life over."
Speaking of sex, have you
noticed that neither the
blunt Anglo-Saxon "fuck,"
nor the scientific-sounding
"sexual intercourse"—while
"copulation" suggests
a math problem—are
adequate to the splendid
act itself? The Elizabethans,
as often is the case, had
a better word, "swive."
Now that's more like it.

Part IV:
Killer Whales Attack Yachts

Killer Whales Attack Yachts Off Gibraltar

They're not budding revolutionaries
out to get the fat cats on deck,
nor is their goal to free the oceans
of all those large sleek interlopers
churning up the waters,
yet gangs of Orcas have struck
hundreds of yachts, sinking
a few, and will not stop.
The cause of this populist revolt?
It's the rudders, stupid.
It seems teenage killer whales
began nosing around these new toys,
bumping their heads and such,
but if you and your sweet sixteen pals
happen to be twelve feet long
you can do a massive
amount of damage.
It's a kind of fad, experts say,
like the time Orcas began wearing
dead salmon as hats (that
was a lot of fun), and this
is just a thrill-seeking game
with dangerous consequences.
And now that Bluefin tuna
are back in abundance
teenage whales don't need
to take all day hunting for food,
this boring period of affluence
leaves them with a lot of free time
on their fins, so why not
see who can smack a yacht
the hardest? Let's even try
to make one dive.

The Easy Life

On the Serengeti you see
so many edible animals
roaming about you wonder
why there aren't more
lions around. They could
feast on at least three
squares a day and grow
enormously fat, their kids
could multiply and do

the same. But it seems
one slab of a juicy flank
is enough to keep your
African lion satisfied
for a while. He'd rather
sleep in sun or shade
than cruise the main drag
for one more fast food
snack, another lunch,

no need to rip open one
more belly, toss entrails
out on the grass. Life
is as good as it gets,
why not kick back,
take a long snooze.
Let the bored lady
lions dream of
sexy Asian tigers.

This Is Not a Kafka Story

You might think that animals
never commit suicide because
what do they know of their own
mortality? That is not completely

true. Once there was an octopus
who was kept in a tank and did
tricks at a circus. When the circus
closes he is left in his container

and ignored. He begins to grow
pale, no longer expressing his
shifting moods by changing
color. One day he performs

his entire repertoire of tricks
for the last time, receives no
response, then stabs himself
to death with his beak.

Jimmie and Sook: A Romance

for William W. Warner

New Yorkers talk of *The City* as if it were
the only one in the country as we Marylanders
do of *The Bay* for similar reasons; when we
speak of crabs we mean the blue kind that thrive
in the marshlands on the Eastern Shore.

To grow large a crab sheds its hard exo-
skeleton made of the same stuff as a fingernail,
this is called molting, which leaves behind
a very soft shell for a brief period of time.
To mate: males must be hard, females soft.

When the time is at hand a randy Jimmie
rises on his tippy toes, extends his arms out
in a straight line, and starts to wave them
before he snaps his body back and kicks up
a multilegged storm in the sand.

A female, or sook, on the verge of molting
gets the message, waves red-tipped claws in
and out and begins to back her prime body
toward her mate, lures him into position on
top of her. Next comes "the grab": he seizes

her, pulls her up into a cradle carry under him.
Some sooks wave helpless arms as if in protest,
yet soon settle down into a compliant posture.
Then the loving pair, or doubler, faces forward,
sets off for a weeklong honeymoon in the rich

eelgrass plentiful near the Eastern Shore where
the deed is done. For hours he inserts two
tiny prongs or appendages into her genital pores.
Afterwards the happy couple do not lie back
and smoke a postnuptial cigarette. Rather

Jimmie will still cling to his sook for several
days until her soft shell is sufficiently hardened.
He then wanders off for another tryst while she
will take her sweet time to deposit her spawn
in some suitable marsh the following spring.

Chesapeake Shellfish

I prefer my fresh oysters
pearl-free with a squirt
of lemon juice, a dab of
cocktail sauce. They go
down easily, the heavenly
taste slips by so suddenly,
it's only fair to have more

straight off the half-shell
on its bed of crushed ice.
Here in the Chesapeake
people in the know admit
those oysters harvested
from the ocean, further up
the coast as far as Maine,

taste better than the ones
from the bay. I'm okay
with those we do have,
plus our famed blue crabs,
especially the sautéed soft-
shells that need no cracking
open and are eaten whole.

Horses and War

God created imperialism
by giving horses dull teeth.
When they chew they pull
the grass up by the roots,

thus destroying their land
for grazing, causing a need
to move to greener pastures,
no matter who lives there.

Horses have eyes on each
side of their head to keep
on the lookout for big cats
and other dreaded predators.

Yet for thousands of years
they were essential in human wars,
since victory was usually on
the side of the bigger horses.

Often wars were started to steal
the horses of some men in order to
fight battles against other men
to gain more horses and land.

It wasn't until World War I
that petroleum replaced grass
as the fuel of war, yet we all
know what happened when

at the start of World War II
brave Polish cavalry rode out
to confront a German blitzkrieg
by a host of panzer divisions.

The Split-Up

Some couples like some
continents I could name
slowly drift apart. In time
separations grow so large
one continent forgets the
other is there and so it
remains for eons until
a wiseass notes how sails
on the horizon sink

out of sight. Another
somebody gets the bright
idea to pay a call on that
other continent and see
if they can let bygones
be bygones and try to
patch things up. They
meet again, exchange
presents, but one isn't

a very nice person and
the couple fight and fight
some more in order to
impose a reconciliation,
yet the battles become so
bloody and bitter it starts
to dawn on thoughtful
people that after all this
wasn't such a good idea.

An Ariel View

From the air it is perfectly clear
that the earth is a jigsaw puzzle
with all the pieces in place even if
they don't spell out words or form
an ideal crazy quilt. Above the heart-
land of America most pieces are
green until the tan deserts of Nevada,
Colorado's gray, snow-tipped Rockies,
the lines below that reflect the sun
and curl like silver snakes across

the land are meandering rivers
that always seem to get where
they want to go. Don't kid yourself,
all this is far too random to be
a part of God's unfolding design.
In our country massive glaciers
scraped out the present shape
of the terrain. Indigenous people
burned undergrowth to plant corn
and other crops, the so-called
pioneers felled entire forests.

Over time farmers turned fields
into vast agribusinesses, towns,
cities, and factories followed,
that's man-made smoke you see
drifting below and sometimes
rising up to join the clouds.

From this high up I don’t have
a cruel or critical word to say
about all this splendor beyond
my comprehension—once we
land on the ground no doubt
my opinions will change.

Big Man on Campus

He is an I-Tappa-Keg frat rat,
a twisted grin on his face
all through the class, naturally
he takes no notes, shambles
out when the bell rings while
I'm in mid-sentence. The odds

of his passing the course are
next to nil. He's one of those
cool guys, finds college the most
challenging three weeks
of his life. His dad is a big
mucky-muck at some Forbes-

listed corporation so he'll
come out okay, even on top,
and if you doubt my word
he will tell you so himself,
find him straddling a barstool
at a local, running up a tab.

An Accident

If the car I'm following weaves
onto a rumble strip, I assume
the driver is drunk and stay back.
Given such frequent erratic behavior
I expect to see more accidents.

When two cars race past me at over
a hundred miles an hour I stare
into the distance for a dark blue
plume of smoke and expect to see
metal twisted like modern sculpture.

Driving a Florida country road
by a field of strawberries, a pickup
in front of me, packed with migrant
workers, suddenly swerves, tips over,
sends people in the back sprawling

in all directions. Two women
stand in a stupor that might pass
for indifference. A man slumps
down in the truck's cab, waiting
for the bleeding to stop. One, back

broken, lies bent on the pavement
as if he had been dropped from
a great height, while howling children
run barefoot around the wreck
stepping on shattered glass.

Good (or Bad) Samaritan?

If you pull a thorn
from a lion's paw
the beast may or
may not be grateful.
In either case, I'd
split the scene fast
and chalk it up to
good intentions.

When you see a man
lying by the roadside you
must quickly decide if
you're a Good Samaritan
or not, who's to say if
the guy is drunk, stoned,
or even shot to death?
How do you respond?

In each case beware of
unforeseen consequences.
Say it's a heart attack,
his pulse has stopped,
should you try to perform
artificial respiration?
What if you've forgotten
how to do it properly,

what if you press too hard
and break a few ribs?
Or you don't press hard
enough and the man's ticker
never resumes tocking
again? It's your play,
as the guys say sitting
around the poker table.

Bass Man

Your true bass fisherman wears
his cap backwards so the wind
hitting his speeding boat
doesn't send it flying out over
the lake where a hungry wide
mouth might take a big bite

out of the brim. His Bronco with
tinted windows, outsized tires,
fog lights popping out like
the eyes of a frog, tows his
sleek boat to a bass-hole bayou.
Blue smoke from big outboards

curls across the lake, blending
with the early morning fog.
When storm clouds gather, darkly
laden with moisture, he knows damn
well it could rain cats and dogs.
He is a patient man even if

the bass aren't biting that day.
His idea of great television is
watching a man in a bass boat
cast his line into a placid lake
and sit there for hours until
the bobbin earns its name.

This Just In

Watching television is not good
for your mental health, moral values,
or personal relationships. In Key West
there are always channels devoted
to sermons by slick media-savvy
smooth talkers with pompadours

and blissful smiles, their mega
congregations pack McMansion
churches upgraded to cathedrals
of the holy something or other—
none of these self-proclaimed saviors
can save your soul.

Famished for factual information,
I turn on the History Channel,
which has suffered a hostile takeover
by Ancient Astronaut Theorists
who find that every archeological dig
digs up more evidence of Experiences
of the Third Kind, extraterrestrial

alien visitations: it's right there in
sculpted figures of men in space suits
on ancient glyphs in ceremonial tombs,
proof positive that those huge stone
pyramids in both hemispheres were
erected to guide flying saucers back
to prehistoric landing sites.

The Poison Kitchen[2]

The *Munich Post* consistently
sounded the alarm about the dangers
of Hitler. Starting in the 1920s
exposés by intrepid journalists
depicted his unstable personality,
perverse proclivities, twisted
ideology, and ruthless followers.
Hitler set out to destroy the paper
he called "The Poison Kitchen."

They ridiculed him in cartoons,
investigated his shady dealings,
detailed his evil designs, including
a "final solution" to send the Jews
to labor camps in remote swamps.
When Hitler's half-niece Geli Raubal,
unwilling object of his obsessions,
supposedly shot herself with his gun
they debunked the official version.

As his henchmen launched
the Beer Hall Putsch—before it
became a fiasco that sent
their leader to prison—they trashed
the offices of the *Munich Post.*
After his release a year later,
the paper intensified its revelations
about secret Nazi death squads
eliminating a hit list of enemies.

---

[2] "The Poison Kitchen" is based on Ron Rosenbaum's acute study, *Explaining Hitler.*

To retaliate, Hitler used both violence
and lawsuits, suing the newspaper
for libel, while reactionary Bavarian
courts often ruled in his favor. His stab-
in-the-back mantra of how World War I
was lost, promises to make Germany
great again, became popular, "Hitler-
smitten women" gave money and jewels,
young men rallied to his nihilistic cause.

Like most megalomaniacs Hitler
was thin-skinned, quick to take offense
and seek revenge. He had a compulsion
to spread false accusations, using blackmail
and extortion to intimidate his opponents.
He found that the more he told a lie
the more people came to believe it.
German politicians thought they could
tame him, but they were wrong.

When Hitler came to power in 1933
the offices of the *Munich Post* were
sacked and burned to the ground,
the reporters sent to concentration camps
where most died. The Reichstag fire
was used as an excuse to destroy what
was left of the free press, other papers
cravenly complied with the Nazi line.

This prescient story haunts me: it shows
what happens when the henhouse elects
the fox, when people, under the spell of
a charlatan promising only he can solve
their problems, hand over unchecked power.
History shows such patterns repeat:
what will be Trump's Reichstag fire?

The Dumbest Crooks

TV loves to do shows about dumb crooks:
one points his finger under his sweatshirt
pretending it's a gun, one tries to enter
a store via the chimney and gets stuck.
Another, cash in hands, keeps pushing
on a door that clearly says "Pull"

until the police arrive. A man at the register
says he has no cash but he will later,
so the thief returns and a cop is waiting.
Asked by detectives for an ID, a crook
displays several. A gang tries to steal
an ATM too large to fit in their trunk.

Another guy comes in a store, fills out a job
application, then robs the place, leaving
the form behind with his contact info.
One dude steals two six-packs, when cops
arrive they find him drunk as a skunk
on a porch directly across the street.

Tattoo Artist

He comes back from Japan
with a dragon tattoo. The artist
says give me some skin, sticks
his barb in with the colors
of choice, sets to his back-
breaking work, graceful circles

are a good way to start. He tells
his canvas not to move, this
will hurt but stay still, there will
be blood, the needle burns
but you'll get used to it,
even come to crave the pain,

beg the artist to go ape, which
is to say epic, on your body,
turn the skin into a text
that keeps on unscrolling—
the most gruesome images
make the biggest impression.

I write this poem because
I too work with ink.

Chopsticks

It makes no sense to eat
rice with chopsticks,
at least as many fall off
as arrive at my mouth.

I'm not sure they're
useful with noodles either,
although a dexterous hand
can get some strands wound

around these thin utensils.
Perhaps the true use for
chopsticks is to slow down
the process of eating,

foster conversation,
savor the available food.
Why not take your sweet
and sour time, let half

the rice slip away, soon
you'll try again until you
snare that last elusive noodle
and clean your plate.

Dining Alone

Nowadays a guy goes to a bar,
picks up a bag of food, goes home,
not a word is spoken, the only
exchange is via credit card.

Often he will eat in his car,
a thing many Americans now
prefer. No more dining rooms
with fresh-pressed tablecloths,

real silverware, napkins large
enough to shield a lap, let alone
candlelight and soft conversation.
Forget first and second course,

an appropriate wine, a tempting
selection of sinful deserts.
From tables to takeaway was
essential during Covid,

yet people still persist
in eating alone, out of sight,
no words spoken, no human
interaction. Try to digest that.

I know, I know, most folks
can't afford a fancy restaurant,
yet eating fast food even faster
sustains neither body nor soul.

Suburban Rites

In the supermarket little old ladies
in a mad rush to get at the cottage cheese
smack her heels with their carts
while she prefers to stroll the aisles,
savoring each item and imagining
scrumptious meals to fix for friends.

While wives pause and purchase,
the pale, abstract faces of the men
drain in the neon as they steer carts
with spectral hands. A gum-chewing
housewife in stretch pants, hair curlers,
slaps a child who shows no surprise,
doesn't bother to cry.

"What did you watch last night?"
one woman asks another in the line
at the checkout counter. When
the cashier pokes the register in
the nose its mouth shoots open.
Each wheels out bags of over-
priced, over-wrapped groceries

including meats of a succulent redness
from a sodium-sulfite rubdown fit
for the barbeque pit and the high caste
ritual of weenie roasts, ancient
pig sacrifices, cooked on a holy altar
of charcoal, consumed in the sacrosanct
grove of a private backyard.

The Need for Trees

Human progress is measured
by taking land away from trees,
cutting them down to clear
the ground and build houses,
plant crops, create fields for
livestock to range and graze.

In the time of the Neanderthals
stone axes gave men a sharp
edge against thick trunks, from
then on humans had their way
with the trees. By Anglo-Saxon
times most of England had been

cleared of its dense forests.
Trees were felled for pasture,
farming, and for hardwoods
to construct various structures
essential for farms, towns,
and city dwellers, to say nothing

of the need for tall masts so
Britannia could rule the waves.
That a lack of trees harms the way
we breathe, our reliance on pleasant
weather, has recently come, too
late, to cross our minds.

Part V:
Curmudgeon’s Lament

The First Philosophers

The first philosophers hung out
in harbors on the Aegean Sea
where men of many minds met
and exchanged ideas about the
nature of things. It was a place
where Asia, Africa, and Europe
came together and mingled.

In spite of differing languages
they managed to communicate,
exchanging merchandise and
metaphysics they talked *back*
to each other and their words
transformed the way we still
think about the world.

Dionysus

Nietzsche defines tragedy
as Dionysian frenzy
within Apollonian form.
He is the god of carnival,
wine, women, and song.

The shallow wine cup
on display in a Munich
museum depicts Dionysus,
drinking horn in hand,
reclining naked in a ship

shaped like a dolphin with
dolphins swimming on
all sides while the mast rising
above a wide white sail
is transfigured into

a spreading vine holding
ripe bunches of grapes
as if in promise that
the supply of tasty wines
will last forever.

Diogenes

The father of Diogenes
is a money changer
who defaces coinage.
The son follows in
his footsteps, finding
conventional leaders
tainted—all those
embossed as generals
and kings that people
accept without
question as good
or admirable—each
one, he says, is
a damnable lie.
Since Diogenes chose
to live like a dog,
he is called a cynic,
meaning "canine."
He lives in a tub,
begs for food
on the streets.
His goal is not
to make the world
a better place
rather surviving
without material
goods and comforts,
steeling himself
against strong feelings
of love, grief, hatred,
or elation, just living
day by day until
the bitter end.

Pythagoras

Following the dictums of Pythagoras
I abstain from eating beans or fallen
fruit. He warns against breaking
bread or eating from a whole loaf,
which creates a kind of quandary.
Don't walk along highways, this
advice makes even more sense
as centuries pass.

In the morning
I practice what he preaches,
smoothing the sheets to hide
the impress of my body, then
remake the bed. We are part
of a cycle. Nothing under
the sun is purely new, each
living thing is our kin.

Long before
St. Francis, Pythagoras speaks
to animals. All of his discourses
are for communal consumption,
he shares his wisdom equally.
Here, have a slice of fresh bread.

Man is the measure of all things,
he asserts, everyone has
their own views and values.
If objective truth does not exist,
is only might right? Yet some
opinions are, if not truer, better.

Nothing is *absolutely* relative.

Socrates

Socrates is at his best
when he tells people
they don't really mean
what they just said.
Think again, his message,

make sure the words
you speak are truly
what you want to say.
If they're not, take them
back and above all

think again.

Augustine's Erections

Q: What did God do before he made heaven and earth?
A: He was preparing hell for those who ask too many questions.
—St. Augustine's idea of a good joke

When Augustine is sixteen
sometimes his penis stiffens
at the public baths. One day
his father notices, smiles,
tells his wife. The prospect
of grandchildren pleases
his parents. He is mortified.
Why does his dick disobey?
Why isn't willpower strong
enough to suppress unwanted
erections? The same problem
at night—impure notions,
emissions minus consent.

He finds himself stuck fast
by the viscous birdlime of lust.
For many years he indulges
his desires, wallows in
sensual and shadowy loves,
delights in the body
of his beloved, relishing
her inheritance from Eve,
sullying clean spring water,
walking in darkness down
slippery paths. Once he
prays, "Lord, grant me
chastity—but not yet."

The question is: if God
is all good, but sex is bad,
where does desire come from?
How can Jesus be a man
of flesh yet pure? Perhaps
evil resides in infants. We are
the devil's spawn, conceived
in the womb of iniquity,
deserving of damnation.

He sees how greedy babies
glare with jealous hatred at
rivals for a mother's milk,
only their feebleness keeps
them from mutual harm.
In sum, from birth our will
is not our own, only God's
strength and grace can save us.

What happens at the public baths
has profound consequences.
St. Augustine's thought shapes
Christian practice and belief.
Who knew so many sins
fit on the head of a penis!

Descartes

Socrates likes to meditate
in the snow. Descartes prefers
to crawl inside a big Bavarian stove
still warm from its last fire. All day
he curls up while a war lasting
thirty years rages outside.

When
he emerges his philosophical system
is almost complete. Snug in
a cast iron stove while all around
death and disaster hold sway
no wonder one might conclude
that identity consists of what
you think.

For years Holland
is the only country in Europe
where free minds can speculate
without fear of prosecution by
Protestant or Catholic inquisitors.
There's something to be said,
after all, for a warm stove.

Sir Humphrey Gilbert Sets Sail

In 1565 the ferocious Spaniard Menéndez
butchers the Huguenot colonists in Florida,
some Frenchmen escape into the forest
and are rescued by an English ship,

brought to London where paintings
of the New World by one survivor,
Le Moyne, stimulate the imaginations
of two half brothers, Sir Humphrey Gilbert

and Walter Raleigh, to dream of colonies.
In 1582 an English seaman named Ingram
is wrecked somewhere on the Gulf Coast
and walks across the vast continent.

Back in England he tells of his adventures:
great plains and huge forests, buffalo,
grizzly bears, panthers, and elephants!—
perhaps he may have spotted one

of the last mammoths then dying
out in the wilderness of Kentucky—
his tales arouse the English to action.
Last seen reading aloud More's *Utopia,*

Sir Humphrey's small ship the *Squirrel*
vanishes over the horizon. His last
words before setting sail are: the way
to heaven is as near by sea as by land.

Virginia

Raleigh names the new land Virginia
for the queen he fails to seduce,
sublimating a generation's lust into
the sweet embrace of a yielding continent
whose rivers offer easy access.
As the queen is barren, so the newly
found land will be fertile beyond dreams
for those heroic enough to have her.

Rivers are wombs, voluptuous waters
where Virginia loses her maidenhood
to greedy men seeking gold and passage
to the Orient. The wanton land's secret name
is Pocahontas, her promiscuous princess,
cavorting with the ship's crew to catch
the desirous eye of John Rolfe, who swears
he marries her to save her soul.

New England

Cape Cod elbows out into the Atlantic,
an arm that beckons, a hook that caught,
a scythe that reaps the saints in sheaves
before their time. At first sight of armed men,

the Indians run into the trees leaving behind
corn fields and burial grounds, their houses
of bent saplings, huge piles of seashells.
As Pocahontas brings tobacco, so Squanto corn,

showing the Pilgrims how to drop a fertile trinity
of herring in each hole beside resurrecting kernels.
They establish their palisaded Utopia
and praise the Lord, quickly developing

an aversion for the very Indians who save
their bodies from starvation. The quest for
the Northwest Passage, the geographical grail,
always ends in a stream's narrowing serpentine

windings or a ship's shallow soundings.
The true wealth of New England lies off
the coast, along aquatic banks, in silver
schools of cod and other feeding fish.

Tom Paine's Bones

"Give me liberty or give me death!"
cries Patrick Henry while his wife
constrained by a straightjacket
screams in the cellar. Tom Paine's
pregnant wife and child die because
she leaves her bed to cook his supper.
His second wife spreads the word
he is impotent. Humiliated, deep
in debt, he flees to London, meets
Ben Franklin, sails to America
seeking a new start.

Common Sense ignites our Revolution.
The king is to blame and plain folk
must fight for their rights. These are
the times that try men's souls—true
patriots, not sunshine soldiers, must
step forward—*We have it in our power,*
he writes, *to begin the world again.*

In France, *The Age of Reason* helps
spark another revolution, not the trust
of Marat and Robespierre who send him
to prison. By mistake a guard chalks
a mark *inside* his open door instead of
outside, sparing him the guillotine.

Back in America he is a *persona non grata*
due to his outspoken Deism. His mind
is his own church, revealed religion is false,
the Bible a fraud. He dies in Greenwich Village,
no Christian burial for him. Instead he lies
in a hay field on his farm under a walnut tree.
William Cobbett digs up the coffin, ships it
to England, stashes it in an attic. After he dies,
nobody can find Tom Paine's bones.

The Spin on Things

In many sports the secret
is the spin on the ball:
the tight spiral of the skilled
quarterback, how the gifted
shooter knows to pronate

a wrist to create the right
backspin on a basketball,
and the talented pitcher
snaps off a sharp-breaking
curve or slider. Even in

soccer you can apply a foot
to add a furious twirl to a ball
finding the far corner of the net.
To say nothing of tennis with
its top spins and drop shots,

or golfers flaunting a whole
cartful of clubs, each designed
to send a whirling orb sailing
a predetermined distance.
Let's admit that it's godlike,

this spin that keeps our globe
afloat in the vast sea of our galaxy.
The whole damn solar system
circles on itself and expands
beyond the reach of thought.

We even like to assume
our little rotating sphere
of a planet has a goal
in mind, as this our world
interminably turns and turns.

Orderly Chaos

Beware the strange attractor
that bubbles in the pot,
makes the smoke curl up
from the butt in the ashtray.
Have you wondered why
the weatherman so often gets
it wrong, or the healthy heart
breaks into wild fibrillations?
Chaos is a far cry from
mere randomness.

High above our heads
a tempestuous ballerina
performs upon a tightrope,
she can leap from point
to point along the rope
but dare not venture
beyond its confine as
we crick our necks to see
how far she dare tilt
lest she slip and fall.

The Brain

1

When early people began to share
their dreams with others, a stimulus
of lasting consequence jolted
the human brain. A baby's skull
must be small enough to pass
through the pelvis, then the brain
has to triple in size to make the life
of the mind possible.

The human body and those of great
apes are remarkably similar,
as they grow older the human brain
grows larger. When an ape's muzzle
protrudes, the similarities are less:
the human skull doesn't harden
nor the jaw extend as much, its
musculature, except for weightlifters
on steroids, differs.

2

Each brain is doing time in
the prison of its skull, but despite
this maximum security the mind
makes a break for it and roams
free in the world, stretches out
to touch a single star, a Milky
Way, a galaxy, even a universe
far more complex than we think,
than we *can* think, yet does
despite the odds.

In sleep, too, the mind slips away
to other realms, strange places
we've never seen before. How
did they get in? How does the brain
stage all these jail breaks? How
can we be fugitives on the run
and trapped in solitary confinement
at the same time?

Free Verse

This verse may be free
but it cost me a lot to write
it this way not that way
by a conscious choice
which is not free either.
We think we make up our
minds but who's to say
who really owns them?
Rather than thinking for
ourselves it may be that
we are thought, tapping
into some collective Jungian
entity that blows thoughts
around the globe like a wind
from which we pick up
this or that vibe.
All this not necessarily in
the present tense, people
were tense in the past too.
You don't have to invent
the wheel although we like
to think we're smarter than
those inferior people living
in caves who did. They sat
around stick fires telling
tales about the day's hunt.
Some lugged huge stones
hundreds of miles across
land and sea to stand erect
in a circle in order to celebrate
seasonal hoedowns. I wonder
if this was before or after
they invented beer.

The Invention of Immortality

What good is knowledge
if it ends with my death?
What has been gained if all
is lost? Not at once but
incrementally, by degrees.
As I age what I have learned

slips from my mind, memory,
to remain wise I would need
to start over but little time is
left. Whence did I come
and whither shall I go?
What does it all mean?

No one wishes to die forever
and therefore we need God,
Unamuno argues, to promise
this is not the case. We invented
God to ensure we will not die
utterly but live eternally.

On the Afterlife

Every being, Spinoza says, persists
in living as long as possible, preferably
forever, which is both absurd and
impossible—what could a bodiless

soul *do* for all that time? Even if
you could enjoy bodily pleasures,
how many hamburgers can you eat?
how many sitcoms rewatch,

when would you stop laughing along
with the canned laughter? Eternal bliss
would bring ever-returning longueurs.
Let's not get into the question of aging,

how many wrinkles can a face take,
what happens after your teeth fall out?
None of us will go on forever—after all,
we only have so much time.

Three Takes on Immortality

1
Who's to say we won't
come back, doesn't the ocean,
in disguise, ascend into the sky
only to return as rain?
And don't creeks, then rivers,
run to the ocean and start
the process over again?

2
The dead are far too good
at staying dead, all this talk
of eternal return is just talk,
some dead people linger
on the Internet for a while,
but I've learned you can't
count on tomorrow, forget
forever, to say nothing of
the Internet.

3
None of us are going
to heaven, but kites are
if you cut the string at
the right moment, let
the wind do its salvation
bit, as they sail out of
sight, while most of us
will sink underground
and, in too short a time,
vanish out of mind.

Comic Wisdom

When the Bible tells us to be
fruitful and multiply it does not
warn us of the subtraction that
lies ahead. Comic wisdom says

the world must be peopled,
hence the need for the classic
wedding plot that ends by
matching up flawed couples

in order to live, not happily
ever after as we like to think,
but to mate and reproduce

so that the all-too-human game
of gain and loss can continue
for generations to come.

Lear on the Heath

(Heath on Lear)

Land cleared of trees and left
to bogs, briars, and bracken
is called "bare heath." The first
human beings are "woodland men,"
homines sylvestres. Human progress
is from the forest to the field.
Heathens are people who remain

on the heath, unfit to be Christian
citizens. They hedge their bets,
you might say, and stay half-wild.
When Lear forsakes his kingdom
he retreats to a bare heath, exposed
to lightning and the pitiless pelting
of a storm, he encounters Tom

and realizes that we are all
poor bare forked creatures
at the mercy of the elements
and our own flawed nature.
Standing on the heath mad
Lear speaks a tragic wisdom
preceding any formal creeds.

Curmudgeon's Lament

What literary reputation I have,
sorry to say, is in remission.
If you are a serious writer in America
seek a goal within reach—neglect.

I've been to Greece, hiked the slopes
of Mount Parnassus; they are littered
with sheep droppings. I will die
the death of a curmudgeon—

sour grapes caught in my craw.
Fame is a game of musical chairs,
who sits or lacks a seat at the table
is willy-nilly a whim of fashion.

As an artist I have cultivated
the art of going unnoticed.
Sometimes in the morning
I forget my own name.

About the Author

William Heath was born in Youngstown, OH. A graduate of Hiram College, with a Ph.D. in American Studies from Case Western Reserve, he taught American literature and creative writing at Kenyon, Transylvania, Vassar, and the University of Seville as the Fulbright professor of American literature. Since 1981, he taught at Mount Saint Mary's University, where he edited *The Monocacy Valley Review*. He retired as a professor emeritus in 2007. The William Heath Award is given annually to honor a student writer. In 2008–9, he was the Sophia M. Libman Professor of Humanities at Hood College. In 2022, he received a Lifetime Achievement Award from Hiram.

He authored many award-winning prose books, including *The Children Bob Moses Led* (Milkweed Editions, 1995; paperback, 1997), which is about the civil rights movement in Mississippi, and *Devil Dancer* (Somondoco Press, 2013) a neo-noir crime novel. His work was nominated for the National Book Award and Pulitzer Prize. His book reviews and essays on Hawthorne, Melville, Twain, William Styron, Thomas Berger, Robert Stone, and Frank Bergon, among others, appear in newspapers, scholarly journals, literary magazines, reviews, and anthologies.

He began publishing poetry in the sixties. His recent collections include *Steel Valley Elegy* (Kelsay Books, 2022), *Going Places* (Kelsay Books, 2023), *Alms for Oblivion* (Kelsay Books, 2024), and *Inventing the Americas* (Finishing Line Press, 2024). He and his wife, Roser Caminals-Heath—author of ten novels in Catalan—live in Maryland.

Website:
www.williamheathbooks.com

www.ingramcontent.com/pod-product-compliance
Lightning Source LLC
LaVergne TN
LVHW090526110826
845146LV00003B/990
* 9 7 9 8 9 0 1 4 6 8 2 2 7 *